TO:

FROM:

D0752558

MERRY CHRISTMAS

AND HAPPY NEW YEAR

THIS COUPON IS GOOD FOR :

_____

_____

_____

_____

WITH LOVE: _____

THIS COUPON IS GOOD FOR :

WITH LOVE:

THIS COUPON IS GOOD FOR :

_____

_____

_____

_____

WITH LOVE: _____

THIS COUPON IS GOOD FOR :

_____

_____

_____

_____

WITH LOVE: _____

THIS COUPON IS GOOD FOR :

WITH LOVE: _____

THIS COUPON IS GOOD FOR :

_____

_____

_____

_____

WITH LOVE: _____

THIS COUPON IS GOOD FOR :

WITH LOVE: _____

THIS COUPON IS GOOD FOR :

_____

_____

_____

_____

WITH LOVE: _____

THIS COUPON IS GOOD FOR :

_____

_____

_____

_____

WITH LOVE: _____

THIS COUPON IS GOOD FOR :

_____

_____

_____

_____

WITH LOVE: _____

THIS COUPON IS GOOD FOR :

_____

_____

_____

_____

WITH LOVE: _____

THIS COUPON IS GOOD FOR :

_____

_____

_____

_____

WITH LOVE: _____

THIS COUPON IS GOOD FOR :

_____

_____

_____

_____

WITH LOVE: _____

THIS COUPON IS GOOD FOR :

_____

_____

_____

_____

WITH LOVE: _____

THIS COUPON IS GOOD FOR :

_____

_____

_____

_____

WITH LOVE: _____

THIS COUPON IS GOOD FOR :

_____

_____

_____

_____

WITH LOVE: _____

THIS COUPON IS GOOD FOR :

_____

_____

_____

_____

WITH LOVE: _____

THIS COUPON IS GOOD FOR :

_____

_____

_____

_____

WITH LOVE: _____

THIS COUPON IS GOOD FOR :

WITH LOVE:

THIS COUPON IS GOOD FOR :

WITH LOVE: _____

THIS COUPON IS GOOD FOR :

_____

_____

_____

WITH LOVE: _____

THIS COUPON IS GOOD FOR :

_____

_____

_____

_____

WITH LOVE: _____

THIS COUPON IS GOOD FOR :

_____

_____

_____

_____

WITH LOVE: _____

THIS COUPON IS GOOD FOR :

_____

_____

_____

_____

WITH LOVE: _____

THIS COUPON IS GOOD FOR :

_____

_____

_____

_____

WITH LOVE: _____

THIS COUPON IS GOOD FOR :

_____

_____

_____

_____

WITH LOVE: _____

THIS COUPON IS GOOD FOR :

_____

_____

_____

_____

WITH LOVE: _____

_____

THIS COUPON IS GOOD FOR :

_____

_____

_____

_____

WITH LOVE: _____

THIS COUPON IS GOOD FOR :

_____

_____

_____

_____

WITH LOVE: _____

THIS COUPON IS GOOD FOR :

_____

_____

_____

_____

WITH LOVE: _____

Enjoying This awesome coupon book?
If so, please leave us a review because we would love to hear your feedback, opinion, and advice to create better products and services for you! Also, we want to know how you creatively you use your book.
Without your voice we don't exist.
Please, support us and leave a review!
Thank you for your support!

Made in United States
Orlando, FL
03 December 2022